Counting Rhymes

Compiled by John Foster
Illustrated by Carol Thompson

Oxford University Press

Oxford   New York   Toronto

OXFORD
UNIVERSITY PRESS

Great Clarendon Street, Oxford OX2 6DP

Oxford University Press is a department of the University of Oxford.
It furthers the University's objective of excellence in research, scholarship,
and education by publishing worldwide in

Oxford New York

Auckland Bangkok Buenos Aires Cape Town Chennai
Dar es Salaam Delhi Hong Kong Istanbul Karachi Kolkata
Kuala Lumpur Madrid Melbourne Mexico City Mumbai Nairobi
São Paulo Shanghai Taipei Tokyo Toronto

Oxford is a registered trade mark of Oxford University Press
in the UK and in certain other countries

This selection and arrangement © John Foster 1996
Illustrations copyright © Carol Thompson 1996
The moral rights of the author and artist have been asserted

First published 1996

British Library Cataloguing in publication Data available

ISBN 0 19 276141 2

10

Printed in China

Letters

One, two, three, four –
Posting letters
Through our door.
Who's got a letter?
Who are they for?

One's for Ali.
One's for Sue.
One's for me
And one's for you!

John Foster

9

Five Old Fishermen

Five old fishermen
Sitting on a bridge,
One caught a tiddler
One caught a fridge.

One caught a tadpole
One caught an eel
And the fifth one caught
A pushchair wheel.

Anon

Hats

A hat for a hamster,
A hat for a dog,
A hat for a goldfish,
A hat for a frog,
A hat for me
To wear in cold weather,
How many hats
Have we got altogether?

Daphne Lister

11

Monsters

Five purple monsters
went out to explore.
One fell down a hole,
so that left four.

5

Four purple monsters
went down to the sea.
One swam far away,
so that left three.

4

Three purple monsters
went out to the zoo.
One joined the lions,
so that left two.

3

Two purple monsters
went out in the sun.
One got far too hot,
so that left one.

2

One purple monster
went out to have fun.
Lost his way going home,
so that left none.

1

Linda Hammond

All Good Dogs

One two three four five six seven
All good dogs will go to heaven;
Purple, yellow, green and red
All good cats will stay in bed.

Carolyn Graham

Spider's Song

One for a cobweb,
Two for the sky,
Three for a ladybird,
Four for a fly,
Five for a beetle,
Six for a bee,
Seven for a centipede
Ready for my tea.

Celia Warren

Just in time for Tea!

Birds in the Birdcage

Birds in the birdcage
Bees in the hive,
One (clap) two (clap)
Three four five (clap).

Dogs in the doghouse
Pigs in the pen,
Six (clap) seven (clap)
Eight nine ten (clap).

Carolyn Graham

One, Two, Three, Four

One, two, three, four, Johnny hiding behind the door.

Three, four, five, six, Mammy catch him, that stop his tricks.

Six, seven, eight, nine, ten, Johnny won't do that again.

Traditional Caribbean,
adapted by John Foster

What Turkey Doing?

Mosquito one
mosquito two
mosquito jump
in de old man shoe

Cockroach three
cockroach four
cockroach dance thru
a crack in de floor

Spider five
spider six
spider weaving
a web of tricks

gobble
gobble

Monkey seven
monkey eight
monkey playing with
pencil and slate

Turkey nine
turkey ten
what turkey doing
in chicken pen?

John Agard

SQUAAWK!

Beach Counting

One for the sun that shone in the sky.
Two for the ships that sailed on by.
Three for the castles I built on the sand.
Four for the seashells I held in my hand.
Five for the points on the starfish I saw.
Six for the crabs that scuttled ashore.
Seven for the waves that I managed to beat.
Eight for the pebbles I perched on my feet.
Nine for the boats that bobbed on the sea.
Ten for my toes that were wiggling free.

Tony Mitton

One Little Kitten

One little kitten
Two big cats
Three baby butterflies
Four big rats
Five fat fishes
Six sad seals
Seven silly seagulls
Eight happy eels;

Nine nervous lizards
Ten brave bees
Eleven smelly elephants
Twelve fat fleas
Thirteen alligators
Fourteen whales
Fifteen donkeys
with fifteen tails.

Carolyn Graham

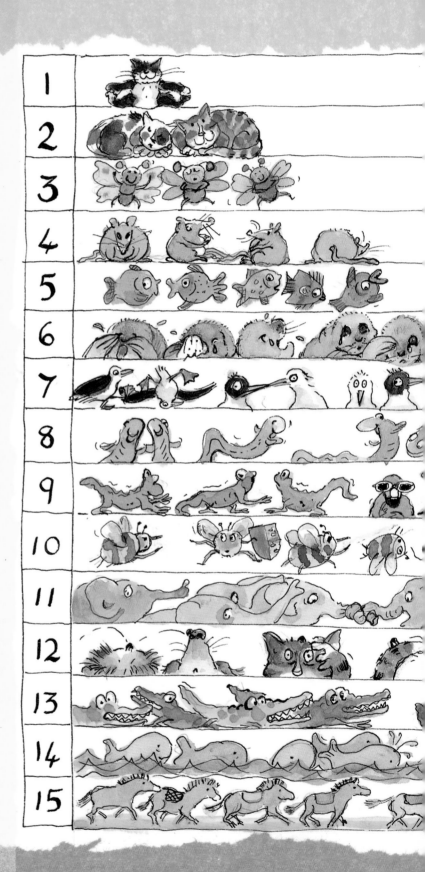

Countdown

Are you ready then?
We start at . . . . TEN!

We're doing fine:
The count is . . . . NINE!

The clock won't wait:
We're down to . . . . . . EIGHT!

Is the next eleven?
No, silly . . . . SEVEN!

Less than two ticks
And now it's . . . . SIX!

Next we arrive
Halfway at . . . . FIVE!

Not many more:
We're down to . . . . FOUR!

Can't stop for tea,
The count is . . . . THREE!

I'm scared, are you?
Yes, but it's . . . . TWO!

Time's almost gone –
We're down to . . . . ONE!

Sorry, can't stay,
It's . . . . ZERO . . . AWAY!

Eric Finney

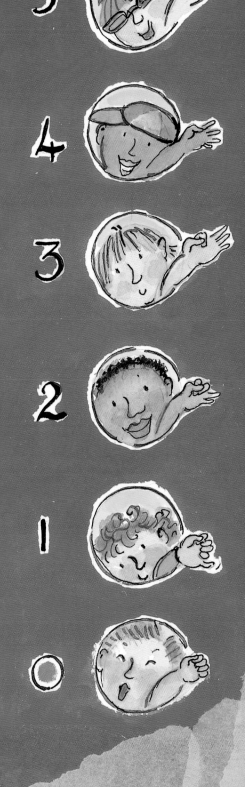

Counting Couples

Well, Noah said, 'Roll up,
two by two.
There's room for a lot
in the floating zoo.'

So the animals came,
and they came in pairs.
They flew in the windows.
They climbed up the stairs.

2 great elephants
heavy and grey.
2 green parrots
with plenty to say.

2 big spiders
with hairy legs.
2 little sparrows
with a nest of eggs.

2 mosquitos,
2 slow snails,
2 quick squirrels
with bushy tails.

Roll up, roll up!

2 of everything
coming so fast
that Noah couldn't count
as they all rushed past.

So Noah said, 'Quick!
There's no time to lose.
If I'm going to count them all,
I'll have to count in two's.

'With a 2 and a 4
and a 6 and an 8,
hurry on in
or we're going to be late.

'2 grey mice:
that comes to 10.
2 more's 12,
with the cock and the hen.

'14, 16, 18, 20,
go on in,
there's room for plenty.
Just keep coming,
(there's no time to lose)
while I stand here
and count in two's.
Ready: 2, 4, 6, 8, 10,
12, 14, 16, 18, 20!
Who's next?'

Tony Mitton

We are grateful for permission to include the following poems in this collection:

John Agard: 'What Turkey Doing?' from *No Hickory No Dickory No Dock* by John Agard and Grace Nichols (Viking, 1991), Copyright © John Agard 1991, reprinted by permission of the author c/o Caroline Sheldon Literary Agency. **Eric Finney:** 'Countdown', Copyright © Eric Finney 1996, first published in this collection by permission of the author. **John Foster:** 'Letters' and adaption of traditional Caribbean poem 'One, Two, Three, Four', Copyright © John Foster 1996, first published in this collection by permission of the author. **Carolyn Graham:** 'One, Two, I Like You', 'All Good Dogs', 'Birds in the Birdcage', and 'One Little Kitten', Copyright © Carolyn Graham 1996, first published in this collection by permission of the author. **Linda Hammond:** 'Monsters' from *One Blue Boat* by Linda Hammond (first published by Viking Children's Books, 1991), Copyright © Linda Hammond 1991, reprinted by permission of Penguin Books Ltd. **Daphne Lister:** 'Hats', Copyright © Daphne Lister 1996, first published in this collection by permission of the author. **Tony Mitton:** 'Counting Couples', and 'Beach Counting', Copyright © Tony Mitton 1996, first published in this collection by permission of the author. **Celia Warren:** 'Spider's Song', Copyright © Celia Warren 1996, first published in this collection by permission of the author.